D0742959

World Soccer Stars ✪ Estrellas del fútbol mundial™

David Beckham

José María Obregón

English translation: Megan Benson

PowerKiDS press™

Editorial Buenas Letras™
New York

Published in 2008 by The Rosen Publishing Group, Inc.
29 East 21st Street, New York, NY 10010

First Edition
Book Design: Nelson Sa

Cataloging Data

Obregón, José María, 1963-
David Beckham / José María Obregón; English translation: Megan Benson —
1st ed.
p.cm. – (World Soccer Stars / Estrellas del fútbol mundial)
Includes Index.
ISBN: 978-1-4042-7665-9
1. Beckham, David–Juvenile literature. 2. Soccer players–Biography–Juvenile literature.
3. Spanish-language materials.

Manufactured in the United States of America

Photo Credits: Cover (left), p. 13 © Denis Doyle/Getty Images; cover (right) © Stephen Dunn/Getty Images; p. 5 © Laurence Griffiths/Getty Images; p. 7 © Shaun Botterill/Getty Images; p. 9 © Vanina Lucchesi/Getty Images; p. 11 © Alex Livesey/Getty Images; p. 15 © Torsten Silz/Getty Images; p. 17 © Mike Ehrmann/Getty Images; p. 19 © Daniel Berehulak/Getty Images; p. 21 © Getty Images.

Contents

Contenido

David Beckham is one of the most famous soccer players in the world. Beckham was born on May 2, 1975, in London, England.

David Beckham es uno de los jugadores de fútbol más famosos del mundo. Beckham nació el 2 de mayo de 1975, en Londres, Inglaterra.

David Beckham started playing soccer when he was very young. When he was 14 years old, Beckham joined the team Manchester United, in England.

David Beckham comenzó a jugar fútbol desde pequeño. A los 14 años de edad, Beckham se unió al equipo Manchester United de Inglaterra.

UMBRO

In 1999, David Beckham won the UEFA Cup Most Valuable Player Award. The best **European** soccer teams play in the UEFA Cup.

En 1999, David Beckham ganó el premio Jugador Más Valioso de la Copa UEFA. En la Copa UEFA juegan los mejores equipos de fútbol de **Europa**.

Beckham is famous for **bending** the ball. He kicks the ball so it curves in the air and falls in the **goal**. Beckham has **scored** many goals in this way.

Beckham es famoso por el **chanfle** que le da al balón. Beckham patea el balón de manera que hace una curva en el aire y cae en la **portería**. Beckham ha **anotado** muchos goles de esta manera.

vodafone

In 2003, Beckham joined Real Madrid in Spain. With Real Madrid, Beckham wore number 23 in honor of Michael Jordan the basketball star.

En 2003, Beckham se unió al equipo Real Madrid de España. En el Real Madrid, Beckham usó el número 23 en honor a Michael Jordan, la estrella de baloncesto.

Real Madrid
BECKHAM
23

Beckham has played in three **World Cups**, 1998, 2002, and 2006, with England. Beckham was team captain for six years.

Beckham ha jugado tres **Copas del Mundo** con Inglaterra, en 1998, 2002 y 2006. Beckham fue capitán del equipo de Inglaterra durante seis años.

ROONEY

In 2007, Beckham joined the Los Angeles Galaxy, a team in the MLS. The MLS is a soccer league in the United States. David Beckham is the most famous player in the MLS.

En 2007, Beckham se unió al equipo Los Ángeles Galaxy en la MLS. La MLS es la liga de fútbol de los Estados Unidos. David Beckham es el jugador más famoso de la MLS.

David Beckham founded the David Beckham Academy. In the academy, children learn that to play soccer, they have to work hard and have fun.

David Beckham creó la Academia David Beckham. En esta academia, los chicos aprenden que para jugar fútbol hay que trabajar muy fuerte y divertirse mucho.

Beckham is a UNICEF goodwill ambassador. UNICEF is a group that helps children. Beckham works to make the life of poor and sick children better.

Beckham es Embajador de Buena Voluntad de UNICEF. La UNICEF es un grupo que se dedica a ayudar a los niños. Beckham trabaja para mejorar la vida de los niños pobres y enfermos.

unicef
unicef

Glossary / Glosario

bending (bend-ing) Kicking the ball so it changes its direction.

European (yur-uh-**pee**-un) Having to do with the continent on which countries like Spain and France are located.

goal (gohl) A frame with a net into which you aim a ball.

scored (skord) Made a point or points in a game.

World Cups (wur-uld **kups)** Soccer tournaments that take place every four years with teams from around the world.

---

anotar Conseguir uno o varios goles

chanfle (el) Efecto que se le da a una pelota para que cambie de dirección.

Copa del Mundo (la) Competencia de fútbol, cada 4 años, en la que juegan los mejores equipos del mundo.

Europa El continente donde se encuentran Inglaterra, España y otros países.

portería (la) El lugar en un campo de fútbol donde se anotan los goles.

Resources / Recursos

Books in English/Libros en inglés

Glaser, Jason. David Beckham. New York: PowerKids Press, 2008

Books in Spanish/Libros en español

Page, Jason. El fútbol. Minneapolis: Two-Can Publishers, 2001

Web Sites

Due to the changing nature of Internet links, The Rosen Publishing Group has developed an online list of Web sites related to the subject of this book. This site is updated regularly. Please use this link to access the list:

www.buenasletraslinks.com/ss/beckham

Index

Índice